Breaking the Power of Manipulation
Exposing the Controlling Spirit

Acknowledgements

    I first want to thank God for giving me the vision and the strength to write this book and to share it with the world. I want to dedicate this book to my mother, the late Vernell E. McDougle. She was a very determined woman that never gave up and in some ways inspired me to do the same. I want to thank my father Arthur Morris for his love and support.

    I especially want to thank God for my husband "Monty" for all his encouragement and standing with me through the good and the bad times. I also want to say thank you to all my friends and family (too many to name). I thank God for you all. I also want thank my pastor Dr. Lance D Watson and The St. Paul's Baptist Church family for their prayer and uplifting words during this journey.

Table of Contents

Chapter 1: The Journey
Chapter 2: It's a Mind Thing
Chapter 3: Identifying the Characteristics of the Controlling Spirit
Chapter 4: Warning Signs of a Controlling Spirit
Chapter 5: Control and Deception
Chapter 6: Are you being controlled?
Chapter 7: Spiritual Abuse
Chapter 8: Manipulation vs. Persuasion
Chapter 9: Breaking Free

Chapter 1
The Journey

It is not my intention in this book to do a comprehensive study on control and manipulation. In no way is this book to be the last word, but this is a personal testimony that I am sharing out of the depths of my heart. My prayer is that my personal experience will be a testimony to God's people to let them know and to recognize the spirit of control. Not only that but also to make them aware that if they are in a controlling situation, that they are not alone and they don't have to stay where they are. I have a real concern for those that have been trapped and ensnared under this kind of bondage because I have gone through it myself. God has delivered me and I want others to know that God is a keeper and a strong deliverer!

My journey begins with my being a part of a ministry that was highly influenced by a leader that was controlling and very manipulative. When I joined the ministry, I was saved for only 7 months and very vulnerable. Within a very short period of time I began to notice things that were going on that were contrary to the Word of God. At first I didn't say anything because I didn't want to question leadership. After about two years of being in the ministry, I found myself feeling like I could not freely make my own decisions unless the pastor was informed first. Actually what happened was that I turned my attention from God and placed it in the hands of others. We were being taught that as long as you take care of the pastor and the church that God was sure to bless you and I believed it.

It got to the point where we were in church six days out of the week and if we did not come to church when we were told that we were not supporting the ministry. It was a way to make us feel guilty and also another way to play manipulating mind games. I worked a full time job and was in school at the time. It was a challenge for me to maintain a healthy balance. I was very fatigued because I was trying to juggle a very hectic lifestyle. After being told that I did not need to finish school because the ministry has need of more of my time, I finally gave up on college and eventually I was let go from my job. I was losing the things that I enjoyed and appreciated in my life. I ended up losing my car and my apartment because I had no job. The church was leasing a building that had two apartments attached. I had no other place to go so started renting one of them. Little did I know, that was really bad decision and to add insult to injury I had to borrow money from the church to purchase my next car. I was stuck between a rock and a hard place now. Now she controlled where I lived and where I went. I had to use my car to pick up those who did not have transportation. And on occasions, I was reminded of how she helped me to get the car. It was just another guilt trip.

I began asking God, "What should I do next?" I finally realized that I needed to redirect my focus back to him and to stop allowing other people to control my mind and my actions. I began to really seek God like never before. I began to read and study the word for myself and consequently was rebuked and ridiculed by the Pastor. I was being told that I thought I was better than everybody else because I wanted a real, authentic relationship with God. God began to show me and give me insight a things that were happening around me. God began to use me to bless other people and He began to open up door for ministering opportunities to preach in different parts of the city I remember one Sunday evening I was ministering at another church and as I scanned the congregation, no one from my church was there to support me like they had promised. At the end of the service my pastor showed up. After the service was over she told me that I sounded a lot like her (as to say that I patterned myself after her). I thought to myself, "I am nothing like you. I don't have any desire to control people to the point that they are paralyzed and operating in fear". Not long after that I heard the Lord speak to me saying, "Your days are numbered here". I went and told the pastor what the Lord said and her reaction was one that I was not looking for. She said that if the Lord was going to move you from this ministry He would tell me first. It was not so much what she said; it was how she said it. She responded with so much rage and anger that I was speechless. This was October of 2003 and in December 2, 2003, I heard the Lord audibly to start packing my things. I said to God where am I going? I had no family there. He instructed me to call me my mother and asked if I could move home. I did just what he told me to, but in the back of my mind I knew that I was not going to be released without a fight. Remember I told you earlier that the apartment that I lived in belonged to the church. The only way out was to move my things in the middle of the night. I was unable to move everything at once so I left some things behind in hopes of going back to get them. To my surprise, when I went back to get my things, someone had changed the locks to the door. I left behind a big screen TV and some valuable items, but I was able to retrieve them. A friend of mine told me that her husband worked for the sheriff's department and he could help me get access to the rest of my things. He actually went to the church while Bible study was going on to let them know that they were unlawfully holding my things and if they didn't give me access to the apartment get in that he was going have to use legal force. I was given an opportunity to get my things but the Pastor told all the brothers that wanted to help me not to. And if they did they were going to be in trouble. How evil is that?

After being gone for about a week I received a call from the pastor, I guess as a one last chance at getting me to change my mind, but it did not work because God liberated me and freed me from being under that spirit of control. Because of my unwillingness to change my mind, during the conversation, she spoke doom and damnation over my life, saying nothing I do would to prosper because I left the ministry. I politely hung up the phone and I prayed that God would help her to see that even though she was anointed, she had no permission to control and manipulate God's people.

My prayer is that my personal experience will be a testimony to God's people to let them know and to recognize the spirit of control, and to make them aware that if they are in a controlling situation, that they are not alone and don't have to stay where they are. I have a real concern for those that have been trapped and ensnared under this kind of bondage because I have gone through it myself. God has delivered me and I want others to know that God is a keeper and a strong deliverer!

My advice to anyone who thinks that he or she is are being controlled is to get out as soon as possible because it does not get any better; it actually has the potential to getting worse. I read a book by Bishop Noel Jones called, <u>Battlefield of the Mind</u> and he said that whatever and whoever controls your mind controls you. In essence what he is saying is that we are to take a serious look at the constant raging war in our minds between the powerful forces that are fighting for control. Not in my own research of the past few years has any validity at all. Sadly, spiritual and pastoral abuse is more prevalent than most people believe. Like child abuse, it often goes undetected, or else it is strongly denied. Spiritual abuse is inflicted by persons who are respected and honored in society by virtue of their positions of religious authority and leadership. When such leaders violate the sacred trust they have been given, when they abuse their authority, and when they misuse their ecclesiastical office to control their congregations, the results can be catastrophic. So choose a church carefully and prayerfully. Remember, not all religion is benign, and not all church experience is beneficial.

Chapter 2
It's a Mind Thing!

Is there really such a thing as "brainwashing," or "mind control"? What kind of person is susceptible? What exactly is a "cult" and how are followers controlled? How can one recognize an organization that engages in such practices, and should such organizations be held responsible for the damage intentional manipulation can cause?

The most insidious threat to our basic freedoms, such as freedom of mind and freedom of speech, is a little-known phenomenon known as mind control. "Mind control" refers to all coercive psychological systems, such as brainwashing, thought reform, and coercive persuasion. Mind control is the shaping of a person's attitudes, beliefs, and personality without the person's knowledge or consent. Mind control employs deceptive and surreptitious manipulation, usually in a group setting, for the financial or political profit of the manipulator. Mind control works by gradually exerting increasing control over individuals through a variety of techniques, such as excessive repetition of routine activities, intense humiliation, or sleep deprivation.

"Cult" refers to a destructive group which uses mind control to deceivingly influence its members. It has become fairly standard to use this term for any organization or group which uses mind control on its members. Cults are not necessarily religious. A cult may form around any theme, such as a political, racial, psychotherapeutic, or even athletic agenda.

For the protection of our basic human and constitutional rights, I hope to provide a fundamental education on the subject of mind control so that you can protect yourself and your loved ones from any individual or organization that is engaging in this kind of manipulation. Satan implemented his mind control scheme on the human race a long time ago and it is time to recognize it for what it is.

Many times when someone is new to a religious organization, he or she is innocently ignorant of the philosophies being taught. It is important to search the scriptures and know for yourself what the Lord has taught. Even the noble men of Paul's time were diligent in knowing what the Bible really said:
"These were more noble than those in Thessalonica, in that they received the word with all readiness of mind, and searched the scriptures daily, whether those things were so" (Acts 17:1

Cults are not only religious in nature, but also are found in a variety of other avenues. You can find cults within music, businesses, and organizations. The word "cult" comes from the word "culture", an integrated pattern of human knowledge, belief, and behavior that depends upon the capacity for symbolic thought and social learning. It is a set of shared attitudes, values, goals, and practices that characterizes an institution, organization, or group, yet in today's society we see cults as dangerous breeding grounds intended for harm. Many times people who are involved in a cult are naïve to what is at the root of their group. Sometimes a cult can be a single family with no church affiliation.

Some cults result in physical harm, suicide or by the attacking of others. Most cults result in isolation from family members and friends, and we must be cautious of modern cults that carry the Christian label.

Some of the most popular, well known, and widely accepted cults are within churches that use mind control to bring their followers into mental and emotional bondage. It becomes so powerful that the followers lose the ability to think for themselves. This kind of mind control involves a severe social influence conditioning program which may include:

- an exclusive system of authoritarian control
- manipulation
- a program of punishment and rewards
- information control
- fraud
- coercion

Depending on the number and intensity of undue influential tactics, and a person's own naivety, one may experience:

- a false personality change
- marked mental or emotional weakness
- compliance
- servitude

Cult-like leaders will keep a person:

- so busy that he or she don't have time for life outside of the cult.

- Many times the leader or cult group will drive a wedge between the family unit by coercing them into separate activities
- drain people of energy so that they are too tired to think about what is happening to them.

Here is a list of things to keep in mind in regards to religious cult

- Control the person's time and environment
- No outside recreation without the group
- Members get positive feedback for conforming to the group's beliefs and behaviors and negative feedback for old beliefs and behavior.
- Good behavior, demonstrating an understanding and acceptance of the group's beliefs.
- The only feedback members get is from the group; they become totally dependent upon the rewards given by those who control the environment.
- Put forth a closed system of logic and an authoritarian structure that allows no feedback and refuses to be corrected except by leadership
- Members are not allowed to question their leaders.
- Flattery is used to puff up the follower in order to make him or her feel accepted and valued.
- Spying on other members and asking for reports on their lives.
- Emphasizing irrational fears about pooaibly leaving the group or even questioning the leader's authority. The person under mind control cannot visualize a positive, fulfilled future without being in the group.
- Instant friendships. True friendships develop over time. Flattery such as "my dear friend" and they really don't know each other very well at all.
- A cult leader will try to persuade you to reduce or eliminate altogether outside friendships and even family.

Some things to keep in mind are:

- It's important for a follower to be able to have the freedom to research about the group without the group leading their research.
- If the follower has been told to refrain from researching about them, then you may want to go ahead and do so.
- An honest group will not be opposed to a follower reading critical information about them.
- If the group has nothing to hide then they will not mind you seeking outside information.
- There is no perfect group, yet anything negative a former member may say should be willingly discussed by your leader. If the situation is covered up or ignored, then be cautious in dealing with this group.

So how can you protect yourself from becoming involved in a cult?

- Know the Bible.
- Question and compare the teaching to the Scriptures.
- Cults who claim to believe in the Bible, but use alternative sources for doctrinal teaching are dangerous. Be sure all the teaching and practices are in agreement with the Scriptures.
- If you believe you are in a cult and are just realizing it, there is help for you.

As 2 Peter 2:1-3 declares, " 1But there were false prophets also among the people, even as there shall be false teachers among you, who privily shall bring in damnable heresies, even denying the Lord that bought them, and bring upon themselves swift destruction. 2And many shall follow their pernicious ways; by reason of whom the way of truth shall be evil spoken of. 3And through covetousness shall they with feigned words make merchandise of you: whose judgment now of a long time lingereth not, and their damnation slumbereth not."

Galatians 1:6-9 says , " I marvel that ye are so soon removed from him that called you into the grace of Christ unto another gospel: Which is not another; but there be some that trouble you, and would pervert the gospel of Christ. But though we, or an angel from heaven, preach any other gospel unto you than that which we have preached unto you, let him be accursed. As we said before, so say I now again, if any man preach any other gospel unto you than that ye have received, let him be accursed."

As it is noted in John 14:6, "Jesus saith unto him, I am the way, the truth, and the life: no man cometh unto the Father, but by me."

The Lord Jesus Christ would not want you to participate in a cult. His expressed desire as put forth in scripture is for you to freely choose Him freely as your Saviour. What kind of relationship would he have with you if you felt forced or coerced to love him?

The Lord Jesus wants us to live in freedom.
"Now the Lord is that Spirit: and where the Spirit of the Lord is, there is liberty. " Galatians 5:1, "Stand fast therefore in the liberty wherewith Christ hath made us free, and be not entangled again with the yoke of bondage." 2 Corinthians 3:17

He is interested in your willing desire to help others come to know him.
"The Lord is not slack concerning his promise, as some men count slackness; but is longsuffering to us-ward, not willing that any should perish, but that all should come to repentance." 2 Peter 3:9

God doesn't want you to give begrudgingly through coercion.

"Every man according as he purposeth in his heart, so let him give; not grudgingly, or of necessity: for God loveth a cheerful giver." 2 Corinthians 9:7

The Lord Jesus wants you to be free from the cult.

"Wherefore come out from among them, and be ye separate, saith the Lord, and touch not the unclean thing; and I will receive you." 2 Corinthians 6:17

Your best defense in escaping a cult is to find help. Breaking free from mind control is not a task that can be easily done all on your own. Some people have broken free from that bondage by weaning themselves away from the group a little bit at a time, while some other seek outside help, and thereby break free immediately and then move away. Whatever the case may be with you, firm support, a strong relationship with the Lord, and a working knowledge of the scriptures are needed. If you feel your knowledge of the scriptures is not strong, find someone who is that is able to help you grow in the area.

Chapter 3
Identifying the Characteristics of the Controlling Spirit

"But I have this against you, that you let the woman Jezebel say she is a prophet [claiming to be inspired] and give false teaching, making my servants go after the desires of the flesh and take food offered to false gods." Rev 2:20 KJV

Who Was Jezebel??

Jezebel was an actual person. Jezebel, the biblical character, first appears in First Kings 16, when she marries Ahab, king of Israel. Jezebel was the daughter of Ethbaal, the king and high priest of the Baal worshipping Sidonians. Baal worship was closely associated with obsessive sensuality and often involved sex acts. Jezebel, as a daughter of this perverse kingdom, was raised in an atmosphere where sex was a path to power and influence.

Ahab, king of Israel, was completely subdued and dominated by Jezebel (a type of modern man). Jezebel then introduced the worship of Ashtoroth to Israel. This god/goddess represented the Canaanite culture of the moon, and was a power-hungry goddess of love and sensuality. Priestess-prostitutes filled her shrines and serviced her worshippers. The lure of these legal, readily available erotic encounters was more than the men of Israel would resist. By Jezebel's influence they left the worship of God for Baal and Ashtoroth. The prophet Elijah laments that only 7000 men in the entire nation were not swayed by her control.

What Kind of Spirit

The Jezebel spirit is born of witchcraft and rebellion. This demon is one of the most common spirits in operation today, both in the church and in the world, and it is a powerful enemy of the body of Christ. She operates freely on sincere believers whose hearts are for God individually, and has also attained positions of power and principalities within the Church. This spirit establishes its stronghold primarily in women; however, many men have been victimized, where it's functions as a "controlling" spirit as well.

The Spirit of Jezebel is basically a controlling spirit working through the lust of the flesh, and the lust of the eyes, and the pride of life. It has, in general, two aims:

1. It seeks to gain identity, glory, recognition, power, and satisfy the need for the "praises of men". This is a consequence of the desire for love and self-worth focused on SELF.
2. The Jezebel spirit seeks to emasculate all men, and divest them of their authority and power over others. It fosters a distrust and hatred of men in general. The Jezebel spirit is in a constant agitation, terribly aggressive, very determined, callous, controlling, selfish, power-hungry, manipulative, unrepentant, deceitful spirit, and an overwhelmingly evil spirit.

There are two main types of the Jezebel spirit:

1. The high-profile type is generally gregarious, outspoken and highly visible. She is often seen as the "woman who wears the pants in the family".
2. The low-profile type is soft-spoken, giving the illusion of being solicitous, motherly, protective, even appearing very submissive. The low-profile type may be the most dangerous, as she is the most difficult to discern. She relies heavily on manipulation for her power, in extremely subtle performances.

Some Characteristics

Within these two main types there are two manifestations: the SEDUCER and the DECEIVER.

1. The SEDUCER uses any type of seduction available to gain control and power, as a method of manipulation but specializes in spiritual seduction to operate on both males and females. Her seduction usually uses subtle flattery and is a form of her seduction is spiritual fornication. Men are particularly blind and easy victims to the subtleties of this seduction, as she flatters them with her attention. Women seduced by the Jezebel spirit are blinded to their own seduction, as they do not expect it, or are not aware of such manipulation.

A good example of the DECEIVER Jezebel personality can frequently be seen as the efficient (and often plain) executive assistant at the side of a powerful businessman or church leader. This type of Jezebel often lacks a gregarious personality, but may be very outspoken and aggressive.

Some of this spirit's features:

Deceiver
This spirit works in "private". People outside her circle hardly know her

maneuvering ways and are an easy prey for manipulation. Those that are possessed by her tend to defend her from any form of criticism.

Man-Hater
Jezebel hates men and majors in destroying them. She cannot have a true godly relationship with men, because her desire is to strip them of all their perceived power and then destroy them, to emasculate them emotionally and spiritually.

Un-submitted
Jezebels revile (despise and show no respect for) authority over her. Building on "dislike of authority" (especially of men since they are frequently the authority figures) coupled with rebellion, she hates anyone placed in authority over her (particularly men), and seeks to destroy them and take their power. Jezebel sees herself as the "goddess on the pedestal".

Power-Hungry
Jezebel is extremely power-hungry, respecting only power stronger than her own. She disdains, or considers herself superior to anyone she perceives as having no power, or power less than she has. She works through her conquest to attain power over others.

Intelligent
This spirit is very intelligent and finds it very challenging to control and manipulate intellectually able people. She is able to manipulate them so well that actually they worship her.

Hard Worker
Jezebels are frequently "super achievers" who are sadly is admired both in the church and business worlds. She is also a master in hindering others from to achieving anything, kind of: doing everything she can to prevent others achieving their set goals for then criticizes them and not having achieved these aims.

Self -Worship
Internally Jezebel worships herself even though externally she may portray a picture of humility and submission. She is very proud of herself and extremely vain, and in her pride talks only about herself. She is usually very attractive and she uses that to seduce her victims.

Jealous
She finds it intolerable when others receive attention over herself and she will do all she can to prevent such from happening. If one gets between Jezebel and the person she is trying to control, she'll attack most viciously, trying her best to destroy the relationship. She will try and destroy one's reputation, undermine

one's authority and, generally, stop at nothing to separate anyone from her intended "victim."

Manipulator
Jezebel uses other people as objects, when it suits her need to gain control, influence and power. Once she has gained the control desired, she generally rejects and tosses the people aside. If they are in her family, she does this emotionally.

Queen Bee
Jezebel demands worship from others (the "queen bee" syndrome). She must have dominance and control in her home. Other family members exist just to please her. Jezebel requires "worship" from her family and followers.

Domineering
The Jezebel is extremely authoritarian ("bossy") by nature, though subtly with the low profile type. She is easily offended if her authority is questioned, and will often respond with extreme anger at even the slightest offence. She demands blind loyalty.

Unrealistic Expectations of Others
Her expectations of others are always unrealistic, because others cannot meet her demand for complete submission. If they do try, she despises them and casts them aside, especially once she acquires what she wants out of them. Anyone attempting to relate to a person with this spirit is literally in a "no-win situation". Nothing pleases this spirit.

Perfectionist
Perfectionism is a common characteristic of the Jezebel, generating self-hatred in the victim She despises others around her who fail to meet her exaggerated standards. This is part of the "unrealistic expectations" she has toward herself and others, but it is also an excuse for disrespect toward others, especially those in authority, since they don't "measure up". So she doesn't have to show respect, of course.

Seduction, Control, Manipulation
Control and manipulation are the strongest parts of the Jezebel nature. These are "spirits of witchcraft" and are extremely dangerous! Nearly everything the Jezebel does utilizes one or both spirits to attain her goal. Jezebel is the ultimate manipulator. The adulterous woman says, "This is the way of an adulteress: she eats and wipes her mouth and says, "I have done no wrong."" (Prov 30:20)

The first step in Jezebel's work is to control her victim by seduction. She will use flattery, smooth prophetic sayings, pleasant words and seductive tears. She views children in a marriage as tools and weapons to manipulate her husband and family.

She knows how to use deep emotional hurts and wounds to manipulate and control, as she creates apparent deep ties with others. Jezebel loves to pull people unto herself and away from those who can truly speak into their lives. Jezebel flows in a whirlwind of confusion and turmoil, where she works best.

Shark

Jezebel is like a shark; she is most vicious and dangerous. She circles the lives of others, looking for teachable, seducible, controllable "disciples" of her own. Jezebel likes to birth spiritual children of her own as she looks for disciples to eat from her own table. She looks for those that are in rebellion, who are weak, wounded, or those who are contending, bucking, and fighting any established spiritual authority.

Possessive

Jezebel is very possessive and domineering; she wants control over others. Jezebel loves power."Give me, give me, give me." You see, money is not really the issue with this spirit; it's power and authority that she's after. She likes to be in control of others' life because she draws her strength from controlling others. She spiritually drains her victims. She uses faults or weaknesses she perceives in the person she is attempting to control to create feelings of shame or guilt, and therefore ultimately submission to her will. She also often uses fear and intimidation to manipulate others into submission under her.

Self-pity

She uses self-pity and her own weaknesses to manipulate another into submitting to her out of compassion or pity. Feeling sorry for Jezebel, is not compassion. It's folly!

Even though often very gifted of the Lord, the Jezebel will frequently operate in the false discernment of the enemy by speaking words of knowledge gained from familiar spirits, and NOT from the Spirit of God. This is "witchcraft." The power of witchcraft is derived from Satan himself and every attempt at manipulation or control "sells out" more to Satan and strengthens the deception the Jezebel is under.

She will even use prayer to manipulate the one she is attempting to control, especially audibly praying over that person to create the illusion, that doing Jezebel's will is actually "obeying God", or to generate fear or other emotion within the person which the Jezebel can then use for manipulation of them.

This is what Rev 2:20 is all about.

Desire for Absolute Power

Jezebels are attracted to people of power like "moths to flames". Often, a very intelligent, efficient, attractive, and even blatant Jezebel can be found serving "at the feet" of prominent leaders, even in the church. The deception and/or seduction of the Jezebel is often so successful that the leader does not recognize who is at his or her right hand. The Jezebel's true desire is to wrest the power from the person being served. If that person is prophetic in nature, the actual mission is to destroy them by any means available (destroy their credibility, undermine their authority, discredit their ministry, cause them to fall into sexual temptation, etc.).

Ambitious
Jezebels are desire to "moving up the ladder" wherever they are, not that ambition is always "evil". It's just another character trait to look for. However, you simply will not find a humble, repentant, democratic and non-ambitious Jezebel.

Convinced
While Jezebel's belief system is obviously incorrect and evil, they are very firmly held beliefs.

Jezebels are usually people of deep convictions. As mentioned earlier, many people controlled by the Jezebel spirit have a true heart for God and earnestly desire to serve him. The original Jezebel [the Spirit is first noted in queen of Israel] was devoutly religious, but was at total enmity with God. She worshipped at the altar of Baal (worship of the flesh). Modern-day Jezebels may indeed believe they are serving the one true God; however, the true hidden agenda is "self-worship." In many cases they have a private interpretation on the Bible, but they will vehemently insist they are correct.

Murmuring, Complaint, and Criticism
Murmuring, complaining and criticism are types of spirits very popular everywhere, especially in the church, and most used by the evil one. She uses criticism of perceived faults in others to build up her own self-esteem, and to j justify her disobedience of, or lack of respect for, others. Because she seeks perfectionism, any fault she finds in others is grounds for disobeying their authority. She uses criticism as a tool to manipulate those around her, and along with murmuring and complaint, causes division to weaken her opposition and thereby to gain control over and to destroy them.

Lustful
Jezebels are "lustful spirits" with lust for power being primary; however, as mentioned earlier, their lust may be manifested sexually, if it will bring the desired result. The manifestation varies from a wife withholding sexual union from the husband for manipulative purposes, to utilizing sexual temptation to draw those more powerful into a compromised position that will cause their destruction or downfall.

Jezebel displays angry, vicious and sometimes violent behavior when opposed. She will turn on the one who refuses to do her will or submit to her (especially if she has been successful in manipulating this person in the past), frequently with a vicious, berating verbal attack aimed at humiliation. The emotional damage caused by these outbreaks can be devastating to the one at whom she directs her wrath. This is often the source of terrible emotional wounds for her children and spouse. When this angry behavior happens in public, it often exposes the true spirit that deceives. Watch for it.

Infirmities and Disease
Jezebels frequently enjoy people's (including their own) poor health, especially the "Low-profile" type. For them, it is a tool for attention, sympathy and other forms of manipulation. The tragedy is that this form of "invited infirmity" eventually leads to real physical problems, and becomes a part of the destruction wrought on the host by this spirit, but it serves to further Jezebel's ends, not to weaken her.

Have you ever felt insecure? Be careful, Jezebel loves to delve in the realm of insecurity. She will spot this in you "instantly" and then the seduction begins.

Destruction
In addition to destroying those around her, because Jezebel especially hates the prey she is controlling (remember the mission of Jezebel is to kill the prophets: the victim is often herself anointed of God to be prophetic), and will ultimately cause her victim to self-destruct. This is referred to as the "Black Widow spider syndrome" since black widow spiders kill their mates. In the spirit realm, there are two applications: First the Jezebel spirit seeks to kill the male authority figures (or prophets). Secondly she seeks to kill her victim, which is mated to her when Jezebel takes control of their life.

Cursing
Jezebels curse everyone, unwittingly bringing a curse upon themselves, most of the time. Criticism is a form of cursing, both of the person being criticized, and of God their Maker. Jezebel is a master of criticism, murmuring and complaining, as mentioned previously. Often those whom she is at enmity with are deliberately cursed in a conscious effort to "punish" and "bring them back into line" to bring them back under her control. Jezebel firmly believes she has right on her side in doing these things, and displays vicious and callous disregard for the well-being and independence of others, having convinced herself that it is ultimately for their good as well and that she knows best and really has their best interests at heart in doing so. Those people who have been on the receiving side of Jezebel's curses feel the anger and the viciousness [other curses acutely and many succumb to them.] However, for those under the "protection of the Cross.", these

curses are most often transformed into blessings instead, leaving Jezebel sapped of emotional energy, frustrated, confused and completely defeated, wondering what went wrong.

Superiority Complex

Jezebels frequently perceive themselves as intellectually and spiritually superior to others, and "talk down " to others. This attitude is actually despising of others.

The Jezebel Spirit absolutely hates and shuns repentance and humility.

These are two mighty weapons, which can be used against her. This is also the key in discerning this spirit -a pride-filled rebellious person refusing to repent.

Jezebel and Fashion

Jezebel is very much attracted to the latest fashion in dressing and she dresses up to demonstrate superiority and literally to "kill."

Bitterness and Resentment

Bitterness and resentment against past hurts and offences are nurtured in the victim by the Jezebel spirit, because she knows a root of bitterness will grow like a cancer and manifest itself in all sorts of physical ailments, which she can use as tools of manipulation, as noted above. Of course, this cancer of bitterness is also slowly destroying the victim. In many cases, the countenance of the victim gradually grows more and more unattractive and in the end, victims controlled by the Jezebel spirit may resemble the very witch- like crones often used to symbolize witchcraft -where this spirit is birthed. The victim rots from the inside out, physically and spiritually, and it shows. People eventually find Jezebel's "Spiritual ugliness" very repulsive. Many Jezebels will be drawn to the most influential Jezebel in operation. Though this is done unconsciously, it has the effect of creating a full-fledged and with a "high priestess" in charge with devastating results!

What about the Spirit of Ahab?

One thing to be noted in these days is that in general there are more women in church than men. This occurs when the "spiritual and natural" head of the family is the woman. Men have the tendency to "run to the hills" when women infringe upon their roles.

The spirit of Ahab is a weak and emasculated figure, indeed the majority of modern men are under that spirit, enslaved to their women. There is an adage that says: "There are two kinds of people in this world: those who rule and those that are ruled, if you do not rule you are ruled".

The couple Jezebel and Ahab represents very well our present society.

It is Jezebel that was the more spiritual, it was her that took the leading role, Jezebel used Ahab's emotional stresses to endear herself to him, it was this woman that drove her husband to do what she wanted, she was ruling the roost in every aspect.

But what happens when the woman takes the leading role that God had prescribed for men?

- If a woman plays her husband's role in directing the family, he will lose his natural drive to bear responsibility.
- When a woman takes the lead, she is playing the masculine role. Unless her husband fights her for supremacy, he must assume second place. And men who are forced into subjection to their wives tend to be angry, dejected and retreat like Ahab.
- When a husband steps into a spiritual role at his wife's command, he becomes vulnerable to her guidance in that role. This is against God's directives and the nature He gave, and often brings conflict in the family and in the church.
- Many men turn their heads when they see their wives stepping out of their God-given role. These men would rather not have to deal with the stone-cold anger they would receive from their wives if they offered any resistance. Have you seen that behavior here and there?

Ahab chose not to notice when his wife worked behind the scenes. Many men turn their heads when they see their wives stepping out of their God-given role. Jezebel knew that she was not the rightful head, so she invoked her husband's name to give her word authority. Did you ever hears it said, "Oh, my husband will not let me do that," when you knew in truth he really would not care? It is a way to maintain control and stop those who would question you. When a woman does this, she stops any ministry God has for her.

Jezebel was deeply concerned about spiritual matters and took steps to help promote her spiritual leaders. In the process, she provoked her husband to destroy those in spiritual authority she did not like. Have you ever seen women influencing their husbands to think evil of those in authority because you did not like something about them? When a woman comes to this place she might as well change her name to "Jezebel."

The fact is that man is made in such a way that he has no defense against the love of a righteous wife, but if he falls into the end of a Jezebel, truly is life will be hell on earth.

Unfortunately for men, there are billions of Jezebels in the world and the once manly men have been reduced to weak type of Ahab's, they have been mentally emasculated and the world is in deep decadence because of that, as we see today.

How powerful is the demon of Jezebel?

For seven years, God had carefully protected Elijah. God fed him in the wilderness. When Ahab's armies sought to kill Elijah, they were unable to lay a single finger on him.

Finally, in a showdown at Mt. Carmel, Elijah called down fire from heaven and resoundingly defeated and killed the priests of Baal. All Israel fell at his feet in repentance worshipping the true God. Elijah was the man of the hour. He was vindicated, victorious, and clearly in charge.

It makes NO sense. Elijah enjoyed supernatural protection for seven years. He watched fire fall from heaven and defeat his enemies, yet when a single angry woman threatened him one time, he lost every shred of vision and ran away. He moaned in self-pity and depression, begging God to kill him! Surely that was a magnificent display of God's power and that power was with Elijah, but at a word from Jezebel he forgot all that and ran in fear. Surely that must have annoyed the Lord at least a little, for it seems that in that occasion Elijah feared more Jezebel that the Lord God.

This is a great example of Jezebel's powerful demonic "anointing" to intimidate, create fear, and cause men of God to withdraw. Jezebel steals our vision. Jezebel will even make us depressed and anxious when there is nothing significantly different in our circumstances. If there are difficult circumstances, this spirit will tell us they are insurmountable, impossible, and overwhelming. Jezebel will make us feel like dying when in reality, we are God's man of the hour.

Jezebel's witchcraft will attack key leaders in her targeted area through intimidation. Those under attack may awaken one morning to find it takes effort just to breathe. All joy seems to depart. Spiritual life seems irrelevant. Demonic voices will echo in our minds "something's wrong with you!" We may suddenly find ourselves in unreasonable anxiety, fearing tragedy or death. Much of what is called "depression" in the ministry is simply Jezebel.

Jezebel wants to paralyze with fear, condemnation, depression, apathy or whatever it takes until we withdraw. The only answer for those under Jezebel's attack is perseverance in battle. We must remain on course no matter how long it takes!

The sad thing is that she is so successful in her endeavor these days.

War

The war continues today between Jezebel and Elijah. Like all wars, there are casualties. Leaders sometimes fall. Soldiers sometimes withdraw. Jezebel wants to keep the church and the world within its present boundaries. She claims to decide the extent of the church locally. We must not tolerate this.

What we must do

First, we must rid ourselves of Jezebel's ways. We cannot cast out lust when we harbor lust in our lives. We cannot bring down a spirit of control if we use manipulation and hype to control our congregations. We must examine our own ways, and repent of Jezebel.

Second, it takes Jehu. Although Elijah was Jezebel's enemy, it took JEHU to trample Jezebel.

Jehu took no prisoners and showed no mercy to Jezebel. He had singleness of purpose and was driven by it. As he approached Jezebel those who saw his chariot noted he "drives furiously" (2Ki 9:20). When others offered peace and compromise, Jehu responded "How can there be peace as long as the harlotries and witchcrafts of Jezebel are many?" (2Ki 9:22)

This is repeated in the NT: "What accord has Christ with Belial? Or what portion does a believer share with an unbeliever?" (2Co 6:15) NO COMPROMISE

Jehu would not rest until Jezebel was dead. Her pleasures could not attract him. Her threats did not deter him. He would not tolerate Jezebel.

Jesus says we too cannot TOLERATE Jezebel. (Rev 2:20) We must learn the prophetic power of the word "No!" We must give no ground.

When Jezebel attempted to captivate Jehu, he did not even allow himself to be drawn into conversation with her. Instead, he called on her eunuchs to cast her down from her balcony. Those with the Jehu anointing will call to Jezebel's emasculated slaves to rise up above their miserable situation, and they too will cast her down, and be set free.

"NO" is the operative word against Jezebel, when those in spiritual authority say "NO" to her, she is ready for war. Remember, Jezebel is a warring spirit who is always dressed for battle.

Brothers and sisters, the time is over nigh, the time is well passed, but we must stand and we must rise up and regain our God given position. What shall we say to our beloved Master, Christ Jesus, when He will ask us: "what have you done with the life I gave you?". There will be lowering of heads and faint voices: "You know, o Lord".

Chapter 4
Warning signs of a controlling spirit Parts 1-3

      The idea of spiritual abuse is not a new phenomenon. In the Old Testament, God spoke against those who operated in their own authority while abusing the very people they were to bless. In Jeremiah 5:30-31 we read, "An astonishing and horrible thing has been committed in the land: the prophets prophesy falsely, and the priests rule by their own power; and my people love to have it so. But what will you do in the end?"

In these verses God is bringing an indictment against the religious leaders of the Old Testament. We see the Lord's anger expressed against those who operate in their own authority. Consumed with their own ambition, these leaders have convinced the people that their power is divine. Yet in reality, these false prophets are merely wielding their self-imposed influence for personal gain, claiming they speak for God.

In Jeremiah 6:13-14 we read again of self-absorbed prophets and priests who are so preoccupied with their own needs being met that the needs of the people are being ignored. We read: "From the least of them even to the greatest of them, everyone is greedy for gain, and from the prophet even to the priest everyone deals falsely. And they have healed the brokenness of my people superficially, saying, 'Peace, peace,' but there is no peace".

A common characteristic of an abusive religious system is that the real needs of the people are lost in the never-ending quest by the leaders for personal fulfillment and happiness.

The tragic story of Diane, a young woman in her late teens who had recently given her life to Christ, illustrates this point. Diane went on a mission's trip with a group from the church she had been attending. One day the mission's team was enjoying some recreation time when Diane suffered a tragic accident that caused her leg to be so severely injured that it was necessary to amputate it.

Diane's parents were not Christians, and in the past they had somewhat resented the amount of time Diane had been spending at the church. When the accident occurred, their response was to blame the church for Diane's injury. They also felt the church should do something financially to help Diane.

During the time Diane was recovering in the hospital, her mother happened to hear the senior pastor of Diane's church describing the new, sporty car he intended to purchase. She began to tell people in the community about this preacher who is living high on the church's money. Word got back to the pastor, and needless to say, he was not happy.

After several weeks in the hospital, Diane was transferred to a rehab facility. While she was in rehab the pastor came to see Diane. Diane was still wheelchair bound because she had not yet been fitted with prosthesis. After the initial greetings and some brief small talk, the pastor bought up to Diane what her mom was saying around town. The pastor advised Diane that her 'assignment' was to talk to her mother and get her to stop gossiping about the pastor. Although Diane was still trying to process the idea of facing the rest of her life without a leg, by the time the pastor left, it was clear to her that her pastor had nothing to say to her to help her face the horrible physical and emotional issues brought on by her accident.

One of the church's staff members made a suggestion that the church buy Diane prosthesis for her leg. Initially, the pastor vehemently opposed the idea. However, after some time, just to help smooth things over with Diane's mom, the pastor reluctantly consented to the purchase. Diane's pastor failed to respond to Diane in a way that honored God. In fact, his response was more like that of the Pharisees of the New Testament, whom Jesus openly confronted concerning the way they treated others. As you read the New Testament, it doesn't take a tremendous amount of insight to see that the confrontations Jesus had were not with tax collectors, adulteresses, prostitutes or other 'sinners.' His confrontations were with the religious leaders and the religious system of His day.

In speaking of the Pharisees, Jesus said, "For they bind heavy burdens, hard to bear, and lay them on men's shoulders; but they themselves will not move them with one of their fingers" (Matt. 23:4). The Amplified Bible paints an even clearer picture. It says, "They tie up heavy loads, hard to bear, and place them on men's shoulders, but they themselves will not lift a finger to help bear them." Jesus is referring to the people being weighted down by rules and regulations that needed to be performed in order to gain the acceptance of the Pharisees. In the same way, many believers today have found themselves crushed beneath the religious baggage of an abusive system. Each day thousands of church members find themselves struggling to earn the favor and approval of a modern-day Pharisee.

Jesus cared deeply about His people and how they were treated. When He saw the multitudes, "He was moved with compassion for them, because they were weary and scattered, like sheep having no shepherd" (Matt. 9:36). The Amplified Version expands on the word weary by saying, "They were bewildered (harassed and distressed and dejected and helpless), like sheep without a shepherd." Notice that Jesus saw them as harassed. This word conveys the idea of some outside force pressing upon the people, causing them to feel weary, distressed and downcast. This outside force was the religious system that placed its emphasis on outward appearances. It was a system that promised peace based on one's ability to follow the prescribed rules and regulations. If one failed, then there was judgment.

Not having a shepherd didn't mean that the people lacked for those who told them what to do. There were plenty of Pharisees willing to do that. It meant they had no one to lead them to spiritual green pastures. A shepherd doesn't drive his sheep as cattlemen drive their cattle. A shepherd leads his sheep to a safe place where food is plentiful and where they can find rests.

Is it any wonder Jesus said: "Come to me, all you who labor and are heavy laden, and I will give you rest. Take my yoke upon you and learn from me, for I am gentle and lowly in heart, and you will find rest for your souls. For my yoke is easy and my burden is light" (Matthew 11:28-30).

A healthy church should produce peace and rest for your soul. Establishing healthy spiritual relationships will always be a challenge, but the process will prevent you from becoming weary and worn, trying to jump through religious hoops that promise God's acceptance and love. If, in order to gain the acceptance of its leaders, your church constantly requires more and more of your life with no end in sight -- and little encouragement along the way -- then you may want to re-examine the church you are attending. God's intention all along has been for the local church to be healthy, life giving, and Christ centered. But because He has chosen to use frail, sin-prone individuals to lead His church, there is always the possibility that a local congregation can fall into deception or unhealthy spiritual patterns.

Warning signs of a controlling spirit Part 2

Opportunities to minister are abundant in most churches. Yet in a controlling church, individual areas of ministry are no longer opportunities to serve. They become necessary in order to prove one's commitment to the organization. Whether it is faithful attendance to worship services or working in some department, proving one's loyalty becomes the key. Obviously church attendance is vital to our spiritual growth. But if we find ourselves attending church so we can win favor with the pastor or to earn his trust, then we have missed the point.

Galatians 2:16 tells us, "A man is not justified by the works of the law but by faith in Jesus Christ." We cannot earn heaven or God's love. The message of God's grace doesn't cancel the need to serve – it just exposes the "why" of our service. Even though we are instructed to engage in certain disciplines in the Christian life, these disciplines are not a means of gaining God's acceptance. They are meant to be a celebration of His unconditional love and mercy.

Fear Motivation

When a pastor tells his congregation that those who leave his church or disobey his authority are in danger of God's wrath, you can be sure this man is operating in a spirit of control. He is attempting to sue fear as a carnal means of keeping people in his church. The line usually goes like this: "If you leave our church, the blessing of God will be lifted from your life, and you will miss God's will." Another version says, "If you leave our church, you will be in rebellion, and Satan will be free to bring havoc into your life."

Fear is the motivation behind such comments -- not love. You can be sure that this type of reasoning is not from God. Jesus never motivated men out of fear. In a controlling church, fear is a form of manipulation. Instead of motivating people through love and servant hood, a controlling church tries to motivate through manipulation. Motivating people through fear is a direct contradiction to 1 John 4:18, which says, "There is no fear in love; but perfect love casts out fear."

Painful Exit

In a controlling church, it is impossible to leave on good terms. Because the pastor's sense of worth is usually based on the control he is able to exert over the congregation, when someone leaves, this insecure leader considers it an affront to his leadership. Therefore he often takes it personally. As a result, when people do leave, they are labeled rebellious, or the rest of the congregation is given the explanation that they left because they had become offended.

In an unhealthy church, there is never a good reason why anyone should leave. Regardless of the situation, the people who leave are always the "problem."

This truism present in abusive churches applies not only to members, but to church staff as well. In one particular church, each time a staff member left, the senior person did his best to cast a shadow over that person's reputation in the hope that it would destroy any chance of that person succeeding without him someplace else.

Tyrone was a youth minister at a church like this. One of the first conflicts he had with the senior pastor took place after a special youth outreach that Tyrone headed up. It was a skateboard outreach. Tyrone went over the idea and details with the senior pastor, informing the pastor that the outreach would require bringing in a guest speaker.

Once everything was given the OK, Tyrone proceeded with the outreach. It was a bigger success than anyone had anticipated. Approximately two thousand kids came for the different skateboard rallies that were held over a period of three days. But instead of being excited about the results, the senior pastor became angry. He told Tyrone that he was unhappy with the even because "it took over the whole church." Tyrone suspected that the pastor felt upstaged by the response. "It was the talk of the church for some time," Tyrone said. Tyrone went on to clarify, "I came on staff there not only to build a successful youth ministry, but also to be mentored in the things of ministry." Tyrone continued by saying that this position was his first ministry position, and he knew he had a lot to learn. But he was willing to do so.

It soon became apparent that the pastor had a different idea concerning Tyrone's position. Tyrone discovered that his job description also involved shoveling the pastor's drive, picking up his dry cleaning, starting his car for him in the winter and cleaning out his pool in the summer. "I didn't mind doing any of that," Tyrone said. "I was just expecting more input from the pastor in the area of ministry." Tyrone continued by explaining, "A lot of the conflict was due to our differing perspectives concerning my position as well as our views about ministry." After about one year, it was mutually decided that it would be better if Tyrone resigned in light of "philosophical differences" between the senior pastor and himself. Tyrone told the pastor that after resigning, he would be moving to Kentucky. He asked the pastor if he could use him as a reference when he applied for another position. The senior pastor assured Tyrone that he would give him a positive recommendation. However, before Tyrone and his wife moved to Kentucky a staff member of the church delivered a statement typed out on the church's letterhead. The statement was an explanation as to why Tyrone was "discharged" from his position as youth pastor.

Tyrone and his wife were shocked. Based on their previous conversation, Tyrone was under the impression that they had reached a mutual decision that being there at the church just wasn't a good "fit." The statement described all the things that Tyrone had done wrong while he was at that church and stated that the senior pastor didn't believe Tyrone was "ministry material." It also said that Tyrone did not have a servant's heart and that the pastor even seriously doubted the validity of Tyrone's relationship with God.

Shortly after Tyrone and his wife arrived in Kentucky, Tyrone heard of a job opening in a church in their new city. He applied in person for the position and left the pastor his resume. Within a few days, they met with the pastor of this new church. He informed Tyrone that when the church board called the previous church about a recommendation, his former church sent the same letter they gave Tyrone before he left. Based on such a poor recommendation, the pastor informed Tyrone that they could not consider him for the position. Shortly after this incident, Tyrone and his wife started a church in Kentucky. Ten years later their church is thriving and healthy.

Many times in an abusive church you will hear the pastor declare curses over the lives of those who have left. Accusations are made against their character, and other members are strongly discouraged from having any contact with the former members. I heard one pastor, while preaching, refer to a former staff member as a spiritual "whore" because he left and took another ministry position in another state. It is true that many people leave churches for the wrong reasons. But in a controlling church, rarely – if ever – is anyone truly blessed by the leadership as they leave.

What Can I Do About It?

How should you respond if your church displays one or more of these unhealthy traits? Here's some advice:

Talk with your pastor or someone else in leadership about your concerns, keeping in mind that if he is truly motivated by a spirit of control you may encounter some manipulation during the conversation. Stay in a humble attitude rather than getting angry or defensive.

A controlling church leader will discourage you from speaking with anyone else about your concerns. However, the Bible says that "in the multitude of counselors there is safety" (Prov. 11:14). Seek counsel from a mature, objective leader in another church or another mature Christian. It is possible that what you have perceived as a controlling attitude may be genuine concern – so pray for discernment.

If after receiving counsel you are convinced that your church is in the grip of a controlling spirit, then you are free to leave. You are not responsible for anyone else who is still loyal to the church, so don't try to rescue them. Pray for those people to discern the situation.

At first you may feel that you can't trust another pastor again, but resist those thoughts and find a healthy church where the life of God is flowing, where the Bible is preached without compromise and where love is evident.

One couple went through the process of leaving an abusive church. The pastor did everything he could to discredit them and malign their character. Initially, they both were frightened that they would be blacklisted from every church in their community. At first, they wanted to defend their character. It seemed that this pastor continued to have control over their lives even after they left. They wondered if they would ever be able to escape his influence.

Finally, they realized that God was their defense and protection. Instead of defending themselves, they decided to pray for their former pastor. The more they prayed for him, the less threatening he became in their minds. The anger they first had toward the pastor was replaced with compassion. As time passed, they realized that he didn't have as much influence as they had initially thought. Because they had kept their hearts pure, they were able to find another church and to continue to grow spiritually.

There is life after spiritual abuse. You may be tempted to feel that you will never escape the controlling grasp of an abusive leader. Satan will cause you to think that the controlling leader's influence is greater than it really is. Don't give in to Satan's intimidation. Trust God to be your strength and your defense. Keep your heart tender.

Pray for those who have used you, and bless those who have cursed you. If you will do these things, you will discover a sure path that God has prepared for you as well as His destiny for your life.

God has a healthy church for you. The Good Shepherd is fully able to lead you into a green pasture where you can grow in your relationship with Him (Ps. 23:2). As you allow Him to lead you, He will also anoint your head with oil, healing any wounds you encountered in an abusive environment.

Warning signs of a controlling spirit Part 3

There is certainly a place for biblical teaching on spiritual authority. But if a pastor preaches on this subject every Sunday, constantly reminding everyone that he is in charge, you can be sure that trouble is around the corner.

In an unhealthy church, the pastor actually begins to take the place of Jesus in people's lives. Commonly, people are told they cannot leave the church with God's blessing unless the pastor approves the decision. The implication is that unless they receive pastoral permission, not only will God not bless them, but they will also be cursed in some way, resulting in sure failure. Controlling spiritual leaders use this kind of reasoning to manipulate people.

We must understand the process a church goes through to reach this point of deception. Because many pastors measure their success through church attendance, they may become disappointed if people leave their church. If they are insecure, they may actually develop a doctrine in order to stop people from leaving. They may preach sermons about unconditional loyalty, using the biblical stories of David and Jonathan, or Elisha and Elijah.

By using examples like these, the leader can actually gain "biblical" grounds to control even the personal areas of his parishioners. A controlling leader may also attempt to instill a sense of obligation by reminding his congregation of everything he has done for them.

This kind of preaching causes church members to seek a position of favor with the pastor rather than a proper desire to "please God and not man." Jesus also condemned such man-pleasing when He told the Pharisees, "I have come in My Father's name, and you do not receive Me. How can you believe, who receive honor from one another, and do not seek the honor that comes from the only God?" (John 5:43-44).

When we pursue the honor of men, we do so at the expense of our relationship with God. If we continue to do so, gradually men will take the place of God in our lives. An unhealthy soul tie is created, and our sense of confidence is determined by our standing with those in leadership. This kind of control will destroy people spiritually! A healthy church will not allow genuine pastoral concern to cross the line into manipulation or control. A true shepherd will use his influence to draw church members into a close relationship with Jesus, who is the only "head of the church" (Eph. 5:23). A true shepherd realizes that the people in his congregation don't belong to him -- they are God's flock.

Unquestioned Authority

In an unhealthy church, it is considered rebellion when someone questions decisions that are made or statements that are said from the pulpit. Granted, there are those who constantly question the leadership in any church -- but often such constant questioning comes from an individual's critical attitude. Pastors must learn to deal with such questioning in a compassionate, positive manner. However, in an unhealthy church, any and all questions are considered threats to the pastor's "God-ordained" authority. Members who do dare to question their leaders or who do not follow their directives often are confronted with severe consequences.

A man from one church told me, "We were told that it is more important to obey leaders than to question what they are doing." He went on to say, "It was unthinkable to question the motives of the pastor."

For example, one couple, members of a church on the West Coast, decided to take a family vacation. This couple purchased their airline tickets and finalized the rest of their plans. They were looking forward to their long-needed time off. Once the pastor discovered their plans, he rebuked them for not getting his permission first and warned them not to go on the trip. They went anyway. Shortly after they returned, they were visited by some of the church's leadership. They were informed that by going on vacation against the pastor's wishes, they were in rebellion. To enforce the pastor's authority, there had to be some form of punishment applied. This couple was then informed that no one from the church was permitted to speak to them or have any contact them for a time determined by the pastor. Even their children were not permitted to play with any of the other children from the church.

Pastors operating under a spirit of control are often convinced that they are the only ones who can accurately hear from God. Under the constant exposure to this spirit, members often become convinced that they indeed need their pastor to think for them. In essence, their personal fellowship with the Lord has been abdicated for a relationship with a man. As a result, they lose their confidence in being able to discern the will of God for their lives.

An Atmosphere of Secrecy

Once a church member surrenders to a system of control, the leader gives limited information to each individual, carefully monitoring each relationship. As a result, each member is only able to relate to other members based on the information he receives from the leader. In this way, if the church staff or pastor determines that one of the members has become a "threat," they have a strategy in place to maintain the control they believe is required. Consequently the church can sever relationships when necessary and keep this process cloaked behind a veil of secrecy.

This is not limited to members of the congregation. I know a pastor who did this with his staff. In casual conversations he would make a comment that would result in one staff member becoming suspicious of another. Or he would say something to cause one staff member to feel superior. This atmosphere fueled selfish ambition and competition among the staff. It became the pastor's way of maintaining control and ensuring that his staff could never challenge his authority. In time, the assistant pastors discovered what was happening, and eventually they all left.

Secrecy may also cloak the area of finances. Pastors may make brazen appeals for money, yet offer no assurance that the finances of the church are handled with accountability and integrity. I have actually heard pastors tell their congregations that the financial decisions of the church do not become a public matter because "the congregation doesn't have the spiritual insight or maturity to understand the dynamics of church finances." Have you heard this line of reasoning?

Some pastors actually preach, "It doesn't matter what we do with your money. Your responsibility is simply to give." However, the Bible commands us to be good stewards -- and part of good stewardship is making sure that proper systems of accountability are established to handle tithes and offerings. (See 1 Peter 4:10.) It is very simple -- money represents power. Ultimately, control comes down to issues of power. Therefore, it should be no surprise that controlling leaders will use unbiblical means to manipulate people into giving.

As good stewards, when we become aware of financial mismanagement, we are responsible for where we sow our financial seed. I can't imagine anyone choosing to continue to give money after becoming aware of the misuse of funds. However, if the approval of those in leadership is more important to a person than financial integrity, that person might still feel compelled to give -- even if misuse of funds was involved.

An Elitist Attitude

The deadly trait of elitism produces an "us and them" mentality. A church with an elitist attitude believes "no one else is really preaching the gospel" except that church. Or at least, no one is preaching it as effectively as they are!

An elitist spirit discourages church members from visiting other churches or receiving counsel from anyone who doesn't attend their church. If anyone visits another church, he is viewed as a dissident.

"Everything you need can be found within the framework of our group," this spirit says, adding, "Everything you need to know, you will receive from the pastor and his teachings." Consequently, there is little respect, if any, for other denominations or church groups.

One individual, in speaking about the elitist attitude within his church, said, "Although we didn't come right out and say it, in our innermost hearts we really felt there was no place like our assembly. We thought the rest of Christianity was out to lunch."

Another man from the same church said, "When a well-known evangelical speaker was preaching in another church in the area, the leaders would discourage us from attending. Also, if the leaders found out that members were considering visiting another church for any reason, they were called in and chastised. 'You don't need to be going to those other churches,' they would tell us. 'The ministry here is rich enough. Isn't the Lord feeding you here?'"

A healthy church respects and celebrates the other expressions of Christ's many-membered body. A Jesus-centered church realizes that no one denomination or local church can win a city, regardless of how large it is. Christ-centered leaders who are clothed with humility recognize that the small church is as significant as the large church, the Baptists are as vital as the Charismatic, and every racial group has a place at the Lord's Table.

A healthy church will promote other churches in the city, rather than simply promoting its own events and agendas all the time. A healthy church will promote spiritual renewal in all churches rather than further the idea that it has some kind of doctrinal superiority. A healthy church will exude the attitude described in Philippians 2:3-4:
"Let nothing be done through selfish ambition or conceit, but in lowliness of mind let each esteem others better than himself. Let each of you look out not only for his own interests, but also the interests of others".

Chapter 5

Control and Deception-How can we recognize them?

The church has become inundated with controllers that will sit beside you on the pew and control your thoughts. Many of these people fall into error and take a lot of people with them. They stir up strife and would have no success if they didn't have people who blindly follow them. I believe that it is a huge problem in the Church today and always has been.

You might wonder; why am I bringing this topic up? Because we are in the last-days, it is important that you think for yourself. You should be submissive to people who are over you in the Lord, but not to the point that you are controlled. You are submitting to their authority in God, their position, but not as if they are a king or a lord over you. God does not use manipulation. Manipulation is witchcraft. God wants us to do His will voluntarily, not because of coercion. By the way, no one has told me anything about anyone that would provoke this topic. I just obey the Holy Spirit. When I do, often it hits the mark in someone. They usually believe that I have discovered some private information about them. Not so in this case.

In this chapter I listed the characteristics of a controller. Here is a partial list. Controllers try to direct your thoughts, so that you think like them. Having your own mind, or making decisions without their input, is unacceptable. They do not want you to be around anyone who is not under their control. The reason is, because they are afraid that you will be taken away from them. Controllers give people what they seem to need. They will find a person who has an inferiority complex and pour compliments on them. It is amazing how effective this is! People that are looking for a father or mother figure will find what they are searching for in a controller. The controller will gently instruct them about every action, as a parent would. They will gradually take over their minds and their lives. People who suffered abuse in their childhood, who come from broken homes, or had parents that didn't give them the proper love and attention, or who were abused in a marriage or other close relationship, are high-risk people for being controlled. They will find a consoling friend in a controller, but at the price of being controlled.

The strange thing is that abused people may be controlled, or they may become controllers. A controller has many of the same symptoms that a controlled person has. The difference is that the controller wants to control their world in order to avoid more pain. The controlled person goes the opposite way. They try to appease their world in order to avoid pain. A controller is easily offended, and will strike out instantly at someone who challenges them. They will scheme and work behind the scenes to sabotage people who are a threat to them. They consider all strong personalities to be a threat to them. The controlled person will work hard to please everyone. They are extremely dreadful of rejection, or of offending someone. Often, they will submit to almost total control that may last for years, or even a life time, before they will risk offending the controller. Controllers recognize a victim when they meet one—and when the two meet, a controlling situation will develop.

The sad truth is that God cannot work through either a controller or a controlled person. Both types of individuals are unresponsive to the Holy Spirit. The controller cannot let go and surrender to the authority of God. The thing that he or she fears most is trust, which is the basis of faith. Trust is a necessary part of surrender, and the controller only trusts what he or she can see, touch, comprehend logically, and control.

The controlled person is often too submissive to an individual to become submissive to God. God cannot work through them because they are listening to another voice. If they try to follow God, they will have to say "no" to the controller. They will also appear to be doing something on their own, and that is one thing that the controller will not tolerate. The controller will discourage them until they quit doing the will of God and began obeying the controller again. Controllers are miserable unless they have someone to control. In most cases they find someone that is willing to submit to them. Although she never confronted me directly for helping her captive to break free, the controller caused much trouble in other ways.

People may ask, "How do I know that I am a controlled person?" One of the ways that you know that you are controlled, or a target for being controlled, is by recognizing how you feel about people. Controlled people are intimidated into obeying the wishes of the controller. Are you afraid to speak your mind? To say, "no?" Are you doing things that you do not wish to do, because you cannot say "no?" Are you always overly concerned about what someone is going to think about you? When you say "no," is there someone in your life that will not rest until they make you change your mind? If you refuse to change your mind, do they become offended? Do they try to dominate you more, or intimidate you into giving in to them? Do they try to "punish" you by being cool or unfriendly? There are many people who are being controlled by someone who is preying on their good nature. Some people are so good natured that they hate saying "no" to anyone. Controllers spot this weakness and exploit it for all its worth. The controller will dominate people who are easily pushed around. If you answer in the affirmative to some of these questions, you may be a target for being controlled or may already be controlled.

However, do not believe everyone is a controller just because you may have a controlled spirit. You might feel the same way around a strong personality as you would around a controller. The difference is, not every person with a strong personality will take advantage of you.

Learn to think for yourself. Recognize the signs of a controller and muster the courage to say "no" to them. If you are feeling miserable because you are being controlled, and are doing things that you do not wish to do, God will help you to break free. It may go against your good nature to just say "no", but sometimes you have to be tough, if you want to be free. Recognize when you are a target for a controller. Change those things that entice them to prey on you. If you cannot say "no" and feel bad about it, you are controlled.

Sometimes we have to practice saying, "I'm sorry, I have other plans," or some other negative. The controller invites you to lunch, but you don't want to go—how do you respond? Practice saying "no" in a creative way, and stick with it. If I want to be with someone, but I really don't have the time, I will say, "Maybe some other time." If I don't want to be with them at all, I politely decline by saying, "I'm sorry, but I'm unavailable." If they persist, I tell them I will call when I am available to have lunch with them, or whatever they are asking me to do. Sometimes I just say "no." What's wrong with that? When is it wrong to say "no" when you really want to say no? There is nothing wrong with saying "no" to anyone if it is a matter of your desires. It is your right as an individual to be able to say "no." God will help you become a stronger person. He does not want you to be controlled by unscrupulous people. If you pray for other needs, why can't you pray that God will help you to be strong when a call you? Don't wait until they have wormed their way into your life. It's much harder to get them out once they have a foothold.

Deception

Someone once said that the most dangerous thing about deception is that it is deceiving. **In my opinion, in the last-days, if we can be deceived...we will be deceived**. But how does one know what type of deception they will be attacked by? There are certain deceptions that I am not susceptible to, but I see other people succumbing to them. However, I have been deceived before by a deception that someone else might easily detect. The good news is that I was able to recover.

In the last days Satan is coming with all unrighteous deception. I have been telling people for years; what ever deception you are susceptible to, that is what you are going to be attacked with. For some people it is lust, in some form or another. For other people, it is anger. Some people battle with jealousy; other ones fight greed, covetousness, or egotism, and etcetera. The point is that we are going to be stricken in the area where we are the most weak. This means that whatever deception that Satan uses against us, we will have a most difficult time detecting it.

For that reason I believe that we need the indwelling of the Holy Sprit to help us recognize last-days deception. Christ said, "For false christs and false prophets will rise and show great signs and wonders to deceive, **if possible**, even the elect. (Mat 24:24 NKJV) This scripture indicates that the deception will be so clever, that it will be impossible for even the godliest saint to detect it without the presence of the Holy Spirit.

I could give people some keys about how to avoid certain deceptions, but there is no way to cover all the things that might attack us. Instead, I tell them that they must pray, must keep the Word of God in their hearts and minds, and must maintain intimacy with God. If a person does not do these things, he or she is going to be deceived. I have watched people fall victim to deception even while sitting under anointed teaching and preaching. How is this possible? It was possible because they did not maintain their spiritual lives. Let me give you one common example.

In a local church there will be all types of people that are at various levels of spirituality. Some of them are carnal and others are more spiritual. Then there is the group that is playing a deadly game with God. This group believes that all that is necessary for them to be spiritual is to convince other people that they are. These people are not spiritual; but they have merely convinced some people that they are. This is deception. Consider the following scriptures.

(Jude 1:3-12 NKJV) Beloved, while I was very diligent to write to you concerning our common salvation, I found it necessary to write to you exhorting you to contend earnestly for the faith which was once for all delivered to the saints. For certain men have crept in unnoticed, who long ago were marked out for this condemnation, ungodly men, who turn the grace of our God into lewdness and deny the only Lord God and our Lord Jesus Christ. But I want to remind you, though you once knew this, that the Lord, having saved the people out of the land of Egypt, afterward destroyed those who did not believe. And the angels who did not keep their proper domain, but left their own abode, He has reserved in everlasting chains under darkness for the judgment of the great day; verse 7 as Sodom and Gomorrah, and the cities around them in a similar manner to these, having given themselves over to sexual immorality and gone after strange flesh, are set forth as an example, suffering the vengeance of eternal fire. Likewise also these dreamers defile the flesh, reject authority, and speak evil of dignitaries. Yet Michael the archangel, in contending with the devil, when he disputed about the body of Moses, dared not bring against him a reviling accusation, but said, "The Lord rebuke you!" But these speak evil of whatever they do not know; and whatever they know naturally, like brute beasts, in these things they corrupt themselves. Woe to them! These are spots in your love feasts, while they feast with you without fear, serving only themselves.

The "spots" will gather around them the people who are unspiritual or carnal. They will snare people who do not maintain their spiritual life, who do not pray enough, are not intimate with God, and in whom the Holy Spirit cannot function. These people live their life by the superficial, regarding symbolism over substance, and are easy prey for deception. They pray when they feel like it, seldom study the Word, refuse to grow and mature in Christ, and feel secure in carnality.

I have watched these weak people follow deceivers and believe that they are following godly people. It is a most amazing, but disheartening, observation. They never consider the fruit, as Christ instructed us to do. They only consider the personality, the flattery, or the well-honed image of godliness. What is even more perplexing is that they will follow these deceivers and at the same time reject a godly individual. If they would stop and consider the fruit they would easily recognize the deceiver. In most cases they will not even consider inspecting the fruit of the deceiver. Why is this? It is because they are so deceived. Like I previously said, the dangerous thing about deception is that it is so deceiving.

The last-days will bring a flood of lying spirits and extremely powerful deception. How does anyone believe that they can survive it without prayer, the Word of God, intimacy with God through the presence of the Holy Spirit? In fact, no one will escape deception that refuses to hear and obey the truth.

It breaks a parent's heart when they warn their children over and over again, yet watch as they make the very mistakes that they warned them about. That is how a God feels when he sees people blindly headed down the path of deception with their eyes and ears sealed to the truth. No one can help such a person. They failed to realize that love for the truth is the only way to avoid the great delusion. When people reject love for the truth to blindly follow a deceiver, they are beyond help. They will have to want to be free, but the instruments of their freedom have been discarded long ago.

This sobering thought ought to make everyone of us consider the state of our spiritual life. We should recognize that we cannot go very long without water, and neither can we do without prayer. We cannot live long without food, and nether can we reject the Word of God. We cannot maintain a relationship with our spouses without intimacy, and neither can we expect to know God without seeking and fellowshipping with His presence. The deception today is powerful to the point of being overwhelming. However, we have been duly warned. God is not going to shake us every day and push us into doing what is necessary to maintain a spiritual life. We have some responsibility in the matter. My sincere prayer is that people will wake up before it is too late.

Chapter 6
Are you being controlled?

Every one in any kind of slavery is in bondage. Any sin or sin habit you cannot get victory over, or haven't gotten victory over, is bondage. But there is also a different kind of bondage. It's a type of spiritual bondage. It's a spirit working through another person that is affecting you. In this message, we are talking about a controlling spirit. People who have a controlling spirit will try to control everyone around them, control their lives, and decisions. They will in general do everything to have influence and power. They want to control their lives (and the lives of those around them), to get things their way. Many people are under the influence and power of someone else with a controlling spirit. It can be a parent or it can be a spouse. It can even be a boss at work.

There are many kinds of people with a controlling spirit. It can even be in the church in the form of a man over others, as someone in a overseer position in a denominational structure, as one that is head of foreign missions, district superintendent, or even a bishop; depending on the denomination. And they desire to control everyone under them for their own purposes and gain. They want to be in control. But whether it is in a marriage, the ministries, in interpersonal relationships, or work, there are controlling personalities and spirits that seek to bring other people under their power, position, and influence. Many men have tried to do this, even leaders over nations, like Hitler or Stalin. All dictatorships and other such people, seek to control everyone around them. But these spirits are all around us. They are working in businesses, homes and churches. Whether it is men in authority over other men, or women over other women; they are constantly working to bring and keep others in bondage. A prime example of that is when a board of deacons who try to control the pastor and the church. When decisions need to be made, nothing can be done outside their say so and approval. Sometimes a deacon would try to control a church and pastor because he is one that is the biggest tithe payer in the church. That's how he got his position to begin with. Look at what David said in Psalm 54:3: "For strangers are risen up against me, and oppressors seek after my soul: they have not set God before them. Selah."

In **1 Kings.21:1-7** "And it came to pass after these things, that Naboth the Jezreelite had a vineyard, which was in Jezreel, hard by the palace of Ahab king of Samaria. And Ahab spake unto Naboth, saying, Give me thy vineyard, that I may have it for a garden of herbs, because it is near unto my house: and I will give thee for it a better vineyard than it; or, if it seem good to thee, I will give thee the worth of it in money." Sounds like a good offer and coming from the king, you would in the natural think that this is a very reasonable offer, and there being no reason why he should not have accepted it. But Naboth was a godly man who could not be bought, bribed or baffled. He refuse to see his vineyard because it was against the law of Moses. It was against God's law for a Israelite to sell his property to a foreigner, a non-Israelite. I think Naboth was a reasonable as well as godly man and who have normally been glad to oblige the king and let him borrow his land, or even to plant something for the king, but he said "I cannot sell it to you because of God's law." Naboth politely refused the king and for the right reason, and Ahab knew the reason was the only right thing Naboth could do and still honor God. He was wrong for still wanting it. (**v.3**) "And Naboth said to Ahab, The LORD forbid it me, that I should give the inheritance of my fathers unto thee." Would you have the courage to resist the king under such circumstances? The earthly land God gave them, for a possession, was considered as an earnest of the heavenly possession; which it represented in type and shadow. Naboth was one of the 7000 who did not bow his knee to the "New Age" religion of Baal that was popular in that day, as most had, and was faithful to God. Baal worship then is as the New Age religion today, that most followed after, leaving the serving of the true and living God. Because of Naboth's godly stand, Ahab gets all bent out of shape. There is nothing like the unbending, uncompromising stand of a godly person to arouse the anger of a wicked covetous person. He storms into his palace and even refuses to eat, and pouts like a little spoiled child. Don't you feel sorry for this poor king who couldn't have his way, like a child refused a toy he wants. Now to add to it, like most people of power and prestige, king Ahab was full of pride. Such people today, like him, hate to come up against a person of holy convictions who will not bend their knee. They don't know what to do with them. They can't control them. You know what I'm talking about. But Jezebel knew what to do. She was a woman waiting for her next victim, ready to strike and show her power and show what she can do. "But Jezebel his wife came to him, and said unto him, Why is thy spirit so sad, that thou eatest no bread? And he said unto her, Because I spake unto Naboth the Jezreelite, and said unto him, Give me thy vineyard for money; or else, if it please thee, I will give thee another vineyard for it: and he answered, I will not give thee my vineyard. And Jezebel his wife said unto him, Dost thou now govern the kingdom of Israel? arise, and eat bread, and let thine heart be merry: I will give thee the vineyard of Naboth the Jezreelite." Hey, aren't you the king. Aren't you in charge, aren't you king over Israel. Stop pouting, I'll give you what you want. Under the pretense of comforting him, she is feeding his pride and lusts, and blows on the coals of anger in his heart, and takes up his cause. Why? She is saying I have everything under control, I know how to give you what you want. Note the "I will". Does it remind you of anything? How about when Lucifer seven times said , "I will" to God in **Isaiah 14:13-15**. "For thou hast said in thine heart, I will ascend into heaven, I will exalt my throne above the stars of God: I will sit also upon the mount of the congregation, in the sides of the north: I will ascend above the heights of the clouds; I will be like the most High. Yet thou shalt be brought down to hell, to the sides of the pit." That's what happens to all with such pride and desire to be in control of their lives and others around them. Jezebel is very confident in herself, as one who has much experience and has been this road before, who knows how to get her way, for she has done it before. This is not the first time she has walked this way of rebellion and power.

Are you under the bondage or control of one with a controlling spirit?. Are you catching the fallout of another being controlled by one with a controlling spirit, and you are being affected by it by no fault of your own. Or you may be recovering from bondage in your past, that makes it difficult for you to trust other people now, and have wholesome godly interpersonal relationships, as God intended, making it difficult for you to trust your pastor or any person because at one time you were under a controlling spirit. [*I know that the things I am speaking about today are real and true for some here, who either were under a controlling spirit at one time, or are under someone or being influenced by someone with a controlling spirit right now.*] Apart from Satan himself, and his desire to control the lives of all mankind, to cause them all to end up in hell with him, we have the story in the Bible of a person who has a very powerful controlling spirit. It's the story of Jezebel, who was a tool of Satan, controlled by Satan, who in term controlled others.

Now the term Jezebel also has been used to describe a lady who wears a lot of makeup, she was the origination of this, and it refers to one who dresses up and makes up like a harlot, one who is seductively painted up, a loose woman trying to entice men. But I'm talking about a different aspect or side of this Jezebel. Even when she made herself up to be attractive and appealing in a fleshly way, it was because of the desire to control others and her situation, and cause things to go her way. And let me say this. This Jezebel spirit we are going to look at and talk about is not limited to women. It is not a female spirit, versus a male spirit, for members of either sex can have this spirit; but today it is far more prevalent in women, as seen in the women's liberation movement and the New Age movement, and worship of the goddess, etc. Satan is today trying to take over possession of every woman, and then in turn use them to control every man. That is what is going on today. And today's women are falling for his lies, and seductive ways, and appeal to be in control of their lives and others around them. It is what I have many times referred to as "a spirit of witchcraft." That's what a controlling spirit is, that tries to control others, whether man or woman.

Now Jezebel not only controlled and manipulates to get her way, but she did it under a religious cloak or covering. **1 Kings 21:9** "And she wrote in the letters, saying, Proclaim a fast, and set Naboth on high among the people:" In proclaiming a fast, it was saying that your house, city, or nation were under God's judgment. She is telling them there is a problem in your city, trouble, and we need to get to the bottom of it, so you must fast and do this. Prayer and fasting was the means of finding out why God was angry and then repenting to stop his anger. It is very dangerous, when people will use scripture and the name of Christ to control others. Their used to be a movement called the "Shepherding movement." It was a means by which some men controlled the lives of others. Jezebel set Naboth up to be tried and convicted by a court of her peers under the cloak of a religious fast. (**v.10**) "And set two men, sons of Belial, before him, to bear witness against him, saying, Thou didst blaspheme God and the king. And then carry him out, and stone him, that he may die." Ultimately this controlling spirit will do anything to get their way. What is so sad here is that she lied and contrived to do it, and she didn't even want the vineyard. She was not a gardener. That's not what it was all about. It was like a game to her. She liked to pull strings. Ahab wanted a vineyard. Jezebel wanted power to control others.

How do you deal with and rid yourself of a Jezebel spirit. The prophet Elijah tells us, for he knew all to well what it was like to be under a Jezebel. **1 Kings 19:1** "And Ahab told Jezebel all that Elijah had done, and withal how he had slain all the prophets with the sword." That refers to Mount Carmel, when the New Age religion came against the Old Time Religion, and Elijah killed 450 prophets of Baal. He wiped them out. Jezebel is angry because she got her authority and power from these false prophets. "Then Jezebel sent a messenger unto Elijah, saying, So let the gods do to me, and more also, if I make not thy life as the life of one of them by to morrow about this time. And when he saw that, he arose, and went for his life, and came to Beersheba, which belongeth to Judah, and left his servant there." So bold before the altar of God facing 450 false prophets, but now that the big contest over, he is drained and tired, and he listens too and gives into the threats of this controlling spirit. For if she truly thought she could kill him after what just transpired, she wouldn't have warned him, but just killed him. But she knew she couldn't. He just killed all her crew. "But he himself went a day's journey into the wilderness, and came and sat down under a juniper tree: and he requested for himself that he might die; and said, It is enough; now, O LORD, take away my life; for I am not better than my fathers." Here he sits, under this Jezebel spirit, and is giving up, conceding defeat at her hand, and is ready to die. Yet here is where God delivered him from this controlling Jezebel spirit. If you are at this moment sitting under a spiritual juniper tree, under the influence of a Jezebel spirit, defeated, being overcome because of this controlling spirit, you can be set fee from it. The Lord Jesus is able to break you free from her bondage. First of all, you can't fight a controlling spirit by your own power or authority. The victory over a controlling spirit has to be won in the spiritual realm through spiritual warfare. "But he himself went a day's journey into the wilderness, and came and sat down under a juniper tree: and he requested for himself that he might die; and said, It is enough; now, O LORD, take away my life; for I am not better than my fathers." Notice that Elijah did not try to fight fire with fire, flesh with flesh. He didn't try to gain control of this controlling spirit in his own strength or ability. He had reached the end of himself, and went to sleep. It's enough. He is ready to die. He is saying, "God, only you can overcome this Jezebel and get me out of this mess." Can I say that this is the very position the Lord wants you to come too, if you are under a Jezebel spirit. When you come up against an attack of Satan, especially when he uses a friend, or even a family member; to attack you; it is important that you be aware, for there is a right and a wrong way to fight it To react in an unrighteous way to an unrighteous person, and fight back in the flesh, instead of the spirit, will not bring victory and deliverance. Remember when James and John wanted to call fire down from heaven?

Luke 9:51-55 "And it came to pass, when the time was come that he should be received up, he stedfastly set his face to go to Jerusalem, And sent messengers before his face: and they went, and entered into a village of the Samaritans, to make ready for him. And they did not receive him, because his face was as though he would go to Jerusalem. And when his disciples James and John saw this, they said, Lord, wilt thou that we command fire to come down from heaven, and consume them, even as Elias did? But he turned, and rebuked them, and said, Ye know not what manner of spirit ye are of." What was this about? They wanted to pass through Samaria to go to Jerusalem, and they said no, we control this territory and you can't go through it. The disciples wanted to fight them by calling fire from heaven, to gain control and get their way. What did Jesus say? You don't know the spirit you are of. You can't fight that controlling spirit of the Samaritans, with the same spirit. It's not the right way to fight a controlling spirit. The Lord let Elijah go into the wilderness by himself, to come to the end of self. If you are under a controlling or oppressive spirit, either directly or indirectly through another person, God's word for you is that you must let God fight the battle for you, and fight it by the spirit and not in the flesh. We are not better than our fathers, who had to rely on God to fight their battles for them. We can't do of ourselves what they could not.

Exodus 14:14 "The LORD shall fight for you, and ye shall hold your peace."

Deuteronomy 3:22 "Ye shall not fear them: for the LORD your God he shall fight for you." When you are in a situation like Elijah most will either give into discouragement and despair or try to run and hide; or they will attack their attacker and try to fight flesh with flesh, evil with evil. You cannot stoop to the level of a Jezebel to fight her on her terms or in her territory and win. If you have a heart for God you will never win this way, she will beat you. In the flesh, only one with a stronger controlling spirit can win, like when a new witch rises up and destroys an old witch to take over a coven of witches. You can't fight them in their territory, or by their spirit.

Here is the way to come to God if you're in a situation you have no control over. **Psalm 35:1-4, 22-23.** "Plead my cause, O LORD, with them that strive with me: fight against them that fight against me. Take hold of shield and buckler, and stand up for mine help. Draw out also the spear, and stop the way against them that persecute me: say unto my soul, I am thy salvation. Let them be confounded and put to shame that seek after my soul: let them be turned back and brought to confusion that devise my hurt… This thou hast seen, O LORD: keep not silence: O LORD, be not far from me. Stir up thyself, and awake to my judgment, even unto my cause, my God and my Lord." You have a choice to either stand on the Word and let God fight you battles for you, or try to fight in on your on, in your own strength, in which you will loose, for Jezebel will beat you every time. After Elijah fell to sleep, he got a wake up call from an angel. This is glorious.

1 Kings19:5 "And as he lay and slept under a juniper tree, behold, then an angel touched him, and said unto him, Arise and eat." Oh the mercy of God, when he sees us lying down in defeat under a juniper tree. "And he looked, and, behold, there was a cake baken on the coals, and a cruse of water at his head. And he did eat and drink, and laid him down again." This second time he went to sleep, he sleep a lot better. The first time he went to sleep, something was eating him up inside, Jezebel. **Psalm 53:4** "Have the workers of iniquity no knowledge? Who eat up my people as they eat bread: they have not called upon God." He went to bed feeling like Jezebel was eating up his soul. But now he had eaten angel food and slept soundly in the Lord, no longer under depression and oppression, being eaten up mentally, emotionally, and spiritually. There is someone here in a similar condition as Elijah was, under a controlling spirit of person, or under a past experience in which you life was greatly effected by the decisions of others over which you had no control or did nothing to deserve. Those people can pass from our lives and yet they can still be a controlling spirit over you if there is bitterness, sorrow or sulking inside, even if they have moved on. Jezebel was no where to be seen in the wilderness, but he was still under her spell.

1 Kings 19:6 "And he looked, and, behold, there was a cake baken on the coals, and a cruse of water at his head. And he did eat and drink, and laid him down again." It was at his head. Oh the practically of this. Elijah was under a physical and mental attack. Jezebel was trying to mess up his head. He wasn't thinking clearly. He has a mental and spiritual lapse and forgot that God could protect him and take care of Jezebel, and he had a heavy heart because of the attack in his mind. So the angel brings Elijah breakfast in bed, something to take care of his headache. And it's a lot better than aspirin or Rolaids. If the devil has been trying to mess up your mind, know the Lord has an antidote for you. This bread and water is a type and shadow of Christ. To some people bread and water may sound like prison food, for someone in a third world prison; but this is deliverance food. Look at it. Jesus is the bread that comes down from heaven.

1 Kings 19:7 "And the angel of the LORD came again the second time, and touched him, and said, Arise and eat; because the journey is too great for thee." You think you can't face that controlling spirit. Yes, the journey is too great for you in the power and strength of your flesh, and you need a little heavenly bread and water from the hand of the angel of the Lord. "And he arose, and did eat and drink, and went in the strength of that meat forty days and forty nights unto Horeb the mount of God." That's some food. That's some kind of meal that will carry you for 40 days, which is a type of temptation and testing as Christ when through in the wilderness. But when you trust in the Lord, and let Him fight your battles, and take your stand with Him, and feed from Him; then there you will find strength to stand against that controlling spirit in your marriage, at your job, in the church. And there is strength to carry you through your journey for 40 days and carry you to the mountain of God. God took care of her, not immediately, but he did, and God can take care of your Jezebel. Jesus can set you free. . . "who the Son shall set free, is free indeed."

Chapter 7
Spiritual Abuse

Spiritual Abuse is not confined to any one specific denomination. I was as intrigued by this as I studied spiritual abuse and how so many websites speak of spiritual abuse in regards to their specific churches. The characteristics are found among many of them. Spiritual Abuse occurs when a person in religious authority or a person with a unique spiritual practice misleads and maltreats another person in the name of God or church or in the mystery of any spiritual concept. Spiritual abuse often refers to an abuser using spiritual or religious rank in taking advantage of the victim's spirituality (mentality and passion on spiritual matters) by putting the victim in a state of unquestioning obedience to an abusive authority.

As I began to research this topic I found that there are millions of people who suffer from this kind of abuse, including myself. I have indeed suffered from this type of abuse. Many people don't even realize this is happening to them. And when they try to seek help, people mark you as a church gossip and disloyal to your leader. Oftentimes husbands won't realize it either and discredit their wives or children as being critical and demand them to be silent about the matter. Men who have their families in a spiritually abusive church will most likely defend their leader over believing their wives, whom they may also label as emotional.

The reason why I believe these husbands will do so is partly because I have seen it in the marriages I know and also because these men are being taught to defend the preacher. Today's modern Christianity seems to have lost its focus on the family.
If you were to conduct an Internet search with the keywords: "Spiritual Abuse", you will find many resources available to educate yourself about how this type of abuse works. I am not going to reinvent or re-write what has already been diligently researched and

written about, but I do want to encourage you. **There is help available and you do not need to remain in a fellowship where you are being abused.**

This is a hefty topic and this may be the first time you have ever heard of such a thing. Even if you don't think you are being spiritually abused, I encourage you to find a few websites and do some reading about this topic. You might discover that you are suffering from this in your fellowship and you might discover things that you know a loved one is suffering from it as well.

Some key points to recognizing spiritual abuse are:

Psychological and Emotional Abuse
- Any act by deeds or words that demeans, humiliates or shames the natural worth and dignity of a person as a human being.
- Submission to spiritual authority without any right to disagree; intimidation.
- Unreasonable control of a person's basic right to make a choice on spiritual matters.
- False accusation and repeated criticism by negatively labeling a person as disobedient, rebellious, lacking faith, demonized, apostate, enemy of the church or God.
- Prevention from practicing faith.
- Isolation or separation from family and friends due to religious affiliation
- Physical abuse that includes physical injury, deprivation of sustenance, and sexual abuse.
- Exclusivity; dismissal of an outsider's criticism and labeling an outsider as of the devil.
- Withholding information and giving of information only to a selected few.
- Conformity to a dangerous or unnatural religious view and practice.
- Hostility that includes shunning (relational aggression, parental alienation) and persecution.

There is an incredible amount of control among leaders that abuse and often times their ministries become cult-like. They refuse to allow other people lead in ministry if they have not declared and proven themselves to be a die-hard follower. They may avoid contact with them in the future and refuse to return phone calls or emails. Leaders are not supposed to lord over God's heritage, but are supposed to be examples.

1 Peter 5:3, "Neither as being lords over God's heritage, but being examples to the flock."

My heart aches for the women who know they are being treated wrongly and their husbands do not protect their wives from this kind of abuse. I realize nobody is perfect and leaders do make mistakes, but when their behavior becomes a perpetual habit that is difficult to confront and/or correct, then I would suggest it is time to look for another fellowship.

You can heal from this abuse and our Lord hasn't missed a thing. He sees everything and He knows your pain. He does not expect you to remain in an abusive situation. He loves you and He has chosen you to receive an abundant life, not an abused life. He already knows we aren't perfect and yet he accepts us anyway. I don't mean that it's acceptable to take advantage of the grace He has given you, but He knows you can't live up to His expectation. This is exactly why He died for you.

Luke 7:13, "And when the Lord saw her, he had compassion on her, and said unto her, Weep not."

Our Lord Jesus certainly has seen everything you have suffered and He truly has compassion for you. Just turn to Jesus and surrender to Him completely. He can fill the emptiness and heal the pain that you have experienced.

Chapter 8

Manipulation vs. Persuasion

According to the Merriam-Webster Dictionary, to persuade is "to move by argument, entreaty, or expostulation to a belief, position, or course of action; to manipulate is "to control or play upon by artful, unfair or insidious means especially to one's own advantage;" and to seduce is "to persuade to disobedience or disloyalty, or to lead astray usually by persuasion or false promises" (Merriam-Webster). Persuasion is neither good nor bad. It is made good or bad by the intentions of the persuader. Manipulation and seduction are both forms of persuasion that are often considered dishonest or unethical.

Persuasion

It is almost impossible for people to avoid persuasion throughout the course of their day. If they listen to the radio or watch television, they encounter advertisements, news media and the opinions and values expressed by announcers, actors, show hosts and advertisers. If they go to work, they are likely to encounter persuasion from their bosses, co-workers, or clients. If they share a home with other people, they are likely to engage in persuasion over what to eat, which television shows to watch or where to go for fun. Persuasion comes in many forms.

All about Purpose: Persuasion, Manipulation and Seduction

Persuasion itself cannot be good or bad. By nature, it is neutral, until the intention of the persuader and the response of the person being persuaded are incorporated into the equation. It is only when put into practice, and responded to that a particular persuasion can be considered positive or negative. For example, persuading a person to eat healthier foods is good persuasion if you are genuinely concerned for their health, but doing so in order to evoke feelings of guilt or shame would be bad. Likewise, persuading someone to ride a rollercoaster may seem harmless unless the person who is being persuaded is convinced to ignore medical complications or go against their will.

There are some types of persuasion that, while they may not always negative, usually carries a negative connotation. Two of these forms of persuasion are manipulation and seduction.

Manipulation

Manipulation is often considered to be a negative form of persuasion because it involves the use of artful, unfair or insidious means. This means that the persuader may use tactics that may not be fair to the person being persuaded or attempt to trick them. One of the most common areas in which manipulation is used is in the church.

How do you differentiate between persuasion and manipulation?

The difference lies in the means we use to persuade. The Word of God is the only legitimate means of persuasion. Legitimate persuasion is cognitive—stirring the mind with reasonable truth. Convincing with tear-jerking stories, histrionics, and emotional outbursts takes an unfair advantage of people and wrongly muddles their thinking. That does not mean we cannot use all the communication skills available to us, but we should avoid playing on people's emotions, even by repeated singing or playing of hymns. These are artificial and should be avoided because they bypass the reason.

Our goal in preaching is to constrain people to choose change because it is reasonable and right before God, not because they have been manipulated into some momentary feeling or action. We persuade them from the Scriptures to choose the right course of action. We do not pile on emotional pressure until they break. We want them to know clearly what the alternatives are and that they must choose.

If after hearing our sermons someone does not know what he is supposed to do about it, we did not reach that person. I believe the legitimate point of persuasion ends with the clear presentation of the truth and must not move beyond that to artificial emotional stimuli for eliciting a response. This latter kind of appeal has produced false Christians and weak believers bouncing from one emotional high to another without a theology to live by.

In 1 Tim. 4:13, Paul writes to Timothy, "Until I come, give attention to the public reading of Scripture, to exhortation and teaching." What he tells Timothy is to read the text, explain the text, and apply the text. That verse is a call to persuasive, expository preaching.

Paul himself was a very persuasive preacher, but he never tried to manipulate emotions to move people artificially. At the end of one of his messages, King Agrippa exclaimed, "In a short time you will persuade me to become a Christian" (Acts 26:28). Agrippa clearly understood the message. Sadly, he made a wrong decision in spite of his understanding.

Ultimately, however, our sermons will only be as persuasive as our lives. A traveling speaker who does not remain in one place long enough for people to get to know him may be able to "fake" it without a consistent life to back up his message(though this is regrettable). Those of us, who preach to the same people week after week, however, cannot do that. Our people know us, and our persuasiveness depends on the quality of our lives.

Paul's preaching was persuasive, but it was his life that won the hearts of people. The Ephesian elders cried when Paul left them, but not because they would not hear him preach anymore. They were "grieving especially over the word which he had spoken, that they should see his face no more" (**Acts 20:38**). The integrity of the preacher's life is a key element in persuasiveness.

Chapter 9
Breaking Free!

There really is life after being controlled and manipulated!! You may be tempted to feel that you will never escape the controlling grasp of an abusive leader. Satan will cause you to think that the controlling leader's influence is greater than it really is. Don't give in to Satan's intimidation. Trust God to be your strength and your defense. There are many times God writes *Ichabod*, "the glory of the Lord has departed," on the door and leaves. It's the best thing for you to leave as well. Do you want to be in a church that God has left? The fact is, for many churches, "Jesus has left the building" long, long ago! But some refuse to believe it!

The preaching continues, the baptisms continue, the singing continues, the prayers continue, the fellowship, the retreats, the conferences, the new faces continue. There will be the periodic, quaintly message or series of messages that you might hear to make you feel good for a while, but before long things will go back to being the same as before. But be not deceived like the rest of them. You will know that after all of the hot air has passed, after all of the smoke has been blown away, that what you are left with will be the same actions and the same words of the same spiritual abuse that had been exhibited, and will continue to be exhibited.

Sometimes staying in these authoritarian abusive "churches", instead of being helpful, only presents a facade as a healthy, non-abusing, caring-for-people "church." Others might think, "*It can't be that bad. If it was that bad, people would have left! Right?*" Leaving does not kill a dead system; it just makes it look as dead as it is. If we choose to live in captivity in these abusive systems, *time will stand still in our spiritual lives*. Physically we will grow older while spiritually we will continue to be treated and abused *like animals*! As many others have done, it's best to leave as quickly and quietly as possible.

Remember, God works in mysterious ways and works differently with each of His saints. He reveals Himself to us at just the right time. For some, it takes a lifetime of deception to appreciate the truth.

God has a <u>*healthy church*</u> for you somewhere.

Try to reconnect with people who already left the "system", because they saw what you now see. Maybe they were former members who you used to have fellowship with before they left. But when they began questioning and *"taking the other side,"* so to speak, and warning you, you thought they were crazy. And the "church" told you to stay away from them. Go out and find them. Search for the people who were caring enough to warn you before they left. They will probably still be caring.

Another couple went through a different process of leaving an abusive church. It was said that the pastor did everything he could to discredit them and malign their character. As it was described, they both were frightened that they would be blacklisted from every church in their community. At first, they wanted to defend their character. It seemed that this pastor continued to have control over their lives even after they left. They wondered if they would ever be able to escape his influence. It is true that whenever someone exposes darkness and subversion inside the Christian establishment, the hounds will come against that person. Whenever someone unmasks Satan's deceptive ministers along with the evil practices of spiritual abuse within the local church, the hounds will be sent out.
They will show their ferocious mouths, and lust and tear and pry and prowl - anything to shut out the Truth!

Remember the incident in Luke 9 where the disciples wanted to call down fire from heaven? Jesus turned and rebuked them and said, "You do not know what manner of spirit you are of, for the Son of Man did not come to destroy men's lives but to save them." I am afraid Jesus would have to repeat these words to a lot of "church going" people today, especially those in "church leadership" positions, because this spirit, the spirit of trying to silence (even to the point of death) anyone who would dare to oppose or expose them, is still very much alive in many churches today.

Perhaps for many others, in God's providence, it might take a longer time to reassemble once again. We all need to be deprogrammed to some degree or another. *For some of God's saints, a long stretch in the wilderness is just what the Heavenly Doctor subscribes.* Do not be discouraged. Learning something the hard way, is many times, the better way. If the Holy Spirit seeks to separate you for a season that He might break you from shackles of "religious abusers", don't let some other "religious leaders" or family members use the "forsake not the assembly" card to keep you in the poison.

Be aware, though because to take this step will invoke Satan's anger like nothing else. If he can keep you inside of this type of church system, he knows that he can keep you spiritually impotent for a lifetime. You will learn very fast just how little interest indeed many of your supposed Christian friends have in God's Truth. Remember, Jesus Christ, the teachings of Jesus Christ, and the followers of Jesus Christ were hated and despised by most of the religious teachers and spiritual leaders in His day. Do you think that anything has changed regarding this in today's churches? Yes. It's gotten worse!

There will be those who seek to hold you back, those from your family, your church, and those among your friends. They will accuse you of heresy, of joining a cult, of abandoning your friends, and family. It will get plenty rough before it gets better. Your choice to live by God's Word will reveal enemies and persecution from sources you never dreamed of. You will be mocked, lied about, and slandered, especially by those in so-called positions of church leadership. This is all that these people know how to do. The very people who are supposedly in the best position to inform their congregations of the truth of this matter turn out to be the very same people who will destroy and silence you.

Just remember to count the cost. If they hated Him, they will hate you also. God will be with you. He will sustain you. So be patient and remain faithful. It will all be for your good in the end. You can do all things through Christ that strengthens you.

God will reassemble you into His body when the time is right. **Paul**, the great apostle, spent some serious time alone with the Holy Spirit separated from the apostles in Jerusalem. **David** spent considerable time living in caves and among the heathen separated from Israel. **Moses** spent forty years separated from His people before He was prepared to lead them out of Egypt. **Joseph** languished in prison for years. **John the Baptist** stood alone in the wilderness for God, because no one wanted to stand with him. **Daniel** ended up in the lion's den alone, because he was the only one who cared enough about God to pray.

My advice to you would be to seek the Holy Spirit and let Him sort it out and make you whole again. The Good Shepherd, in His good time, is fully able to lead you into a green pasture where you can grow in your relationship with Him, wherever that may be. Blessings and peace be unto you.

Scriptures to Consider

2 Timothy 3:1-5

But understand this, that in the last days there will come times of difficulty. For people will be lovers of self, lovers of money, proud, arrogant, abusive, disobedient to their parents, ungrateful, unholy, heartless, unappeasable, slanderous, without self-control, brutal, not loving good, treacherous, reckless, swollen with conceit, lovers of pleasure rather than lovers of God, having the appearance of godliness, but denying its power. Avoid such people.

1 John 4:20

If anyone says, "I love God," and hates his brother, he is a liar; for he who does not love his brother whom he has seen cannot love God whom he has not seen.

Ephesians 6:10-18

Finally, be strong in the Lord and in the strength of his might. Put on the whole armor of God, that you may be able to stand against the schemes of the devil. For we do not wrestle against flesh and blood, but against the rulers, against the authorities, against the cosmic powers over this present darkness, against the spiritual forces of evil in the heavenly places. Therefore take up the whole armor of God, that you may be able to withstand in the evil day, and having done all, to stand firm. Stand therefore, having fastened on the belt of truth, and having put on the breastplate of righteousness, ...

Galatians 2:4

Yet because of false brothers secretly brought in—who slipped in to spy out our freedom that we have in Christ Jesus, so that they might bring us into slavery—

Galatians 5:1

For freedom Christ has set us free; stand firm therefore, and do not submit again to a yoke of slavery.

Matthew 4:1-3

Then Jesus was led up by the Spirit into the wilderness to be tempted by the devil. And after fasting forty days and forty nights, he was hungry. And the tempter came and said to him, "If you are the Son of God, command these stones to become loaves of bread." But he answered, "It is written, "'Man shall not live by bread alone, but by every word that comes from the mouth of God.'" Then the devil took him to the holy city and set him on the pinnacle of the temple Now the Spirit expressly says that in later times some will depart from the faith by devoting themselves to deceitful spirits and teachings of demons…

Made in the USA
Middletown, DE
20 May 2015